A *Special* Gift

_____

for

_____

from

_____

date

A Personal *Note* Just for You

_____

_____

_____

_____

_____

_____

_____

_____

_____

_____

_____

_____

_____

_____

_____

_____

God's
Promises®
for the
Teacher

JACK COUNTRYMAN

Published in Nashville, Tennessee, by Thomas Nelson®. Thomas Nelson is a trademark of Thomas Nelson, Inc.

Cover design by LeftCoast Design, Portland, Oregon.

Thomas Nelson, Inc., titles may be purchased in bulk for educational, business, fund-raising, or sales promotional use. For information, please e-mail SpecialMarkets@ThomasNelson.com.

Scripture quotations are taken from THE NEW KING JAMES VERSION® © 1982 Thomas Nelson, Inc. Used by permission. All rights reserved.

ISBN-13: 978-1-4003-1839-1

Printed in China

14 15 16 17 18 DSC 6 5 4 3 2

www.thomasnelson.com

Table of Contents

A *Teacher* Is . . .

a person with wisdom who teaches truth, who builds character, honesty, and integrity, and who gives each student an inner compass to know what to do.

a person whose heart is filled with joy at the opportunity for making learning fun, and who loves teaching and creating special moments for learning and exploring the unknown.

a person with compassion for those with special needs; a person who helps them overcome the challenges that may hinder their success.

a person who is generous, gives far beyond what is required, and cares about lives that may someday change the world.

a person with great passion for the task they've been given; to instill confidence and determination to rise above what others may think impossible.

a person with patience when times are not easy, wanting the best for each student and believing in those they have been given to teach.

a person who loves God and looks to Him for wisdom, guidance, and understanding; whose priority is honoring Him above all else.

Through your example, others will see the light that only Christ can give.

—Jack Countryman

God
Promises His . . .

God Promises His . . .

Love

Now hope does not disappoint, because the love of God has been poured out in our hearts by the Holy Spirit who was given to us.

Romans 5:5

Beloved, let us love one another, for love is of God; and everyone who loves is born of God and knows God. He who does not love does not know God, for God is love. In this the love of God was manifested toward us, that God has sent His only begotten Son into the world, that we might live through Him. In this is love, not that we loved God, but that He loved us and sent His Son to be the propitiation for our sins. Beloved, if God so loved us, we also ought to love one another.

1 John 4:7–11

But whoever keeps His word, truly the love of God is perfected in him. By this we know that we are in Him. He who says he abides in Him ought himself also to walk just as He walked.

1 John 2:5–6

For this is the love of God, that we keep His commandments. And His commandments are not burdensome.

1 John 5:3

For God so loved the world that He gave His only begotten Son, that whoever believes in Him should not perish but have everlasting life.

John 3:16

For if what is passing away was glorious, what remains is much more glorious.

2 Corinthians 3:11

"As the Father loved Me, I also have loved you; abide in My love."

John 15:9

God Promises His . . .

Grace

For the LORD God is a sun and shield;
   The LORD will give grace and glory;
No good thing will He withhold
   From those who walk uprightly.

Psalm 84:11

Concerning this thing I pleaded with the Lord three times that it might depart from me. And He said to me, "My grace is sufficient for you, for My strength is made perfect in weakness." Therefore most gladly I will rather boast in my infirmities, that the power of Christ may rest upon me. Therefore I take pleasure in infirmities, in reproaches, in needs, in persecutions, in distresses, for Christ's sake. For when I am weak, then I am strong.

2 Corinthians 12:8–10

But to each one of us grace was given according to the measure of Christ's gift.

Ephesians 4:7

For the grace of God that brings salvation has appeared to all men, teaching us that, denying ungodliness and worldly lusts, we should live soberly, righteously, and godly in the present age, looking for the blessed hope and glorious appearing of our great God and Savior Jesus Christ, who gave Himself for us, that He might redeem us from every lawless deed and purify for Himself His own special people, zealous for good works.

Titus 2:11–14

But God, who is rich in mercy, because of His great love with which He loved us . . . and raised us up together, and made us sit together in the heavenly places in Christ Jesus, that in the ages to come He might show the exceeding riches of His grace in His kindness toward us in Christ Jesus. For by grace you have been saved through faith, and that not of yourselves; it is the gift of God.

Ephesians 2:4, 6–8

Therefore, brethren, stand fast and hold the traditions which you were taught, whether by word or our epistle. Now may our Lord Jesus Christ Himself, and our God and Father, who has loved us and given us everlasting consolation and good hope by grace, comfort your hearts and establish you in every good word and work.

2 Thessalonians 2:15–17

But when the kindness and the love of God our Savior toward man appeared, not by works of righteousness which we have done, but according to His mercy He saved us, through the washing of regeneration and renewing of the Holy Spirit, whom He poured out on us abundantly through Jesus Christ our Savior, that having been justified by His grace we should become heirs according to the hope of eternal life.

Titus 3:4–7

God Promises His . . .

Mercy

Oh, give thanks to the LORD, for He is good!
  For His mercy endures forever.

1 Chronicles 16:34

For He says to Moses, "I will have mercy on whomever I will have mercy, and I will have compassion on whomever I will have compassion." So then it is not of him who wills, nor of him who runs, but of God who shows mercy.

Romans 9:15–16

For the gifts and the calling of God are irrevocable. For as you were once disobedient to God, yet have now obtained mercy through their disobedience, even so these also have now been disobedient, that through the mercy shown you they also may obtain mercy. For God has committed them all to disobedience, that He might have mercy on all.

Romans 11:29–32

Praise the LORD!
  Oh, give thanks to the LORD, for He is good!
  For His mercy endures forever.

Psalm 106:1–3

Have mercy upon me, O God,
  According to Your lovingkindness;
  According to the multitude of Your tender mercies,
  Blot out my transgressions.
Wash me thoroughly from my iniquity,
  And cleanse me from my sin.
For I acknowledge my transgressions,
  And my sin is always before me.

Psalm 51:1–3

Oh, give thanks to the LORD, for He is good!
  For His mercy endures forever.
Let the redeemed of the LORD say so,
  Whom He has redeemed from the hand of the enemy,
And gathered out of the lands,
  From the east and from the west,
  From the north and from the south.

Psalm 107:1–3

God Promises His . . .

Blessings

The lips of the righteous feed many,
    But fools die for lack of wisdom.
The blessing of the LORD makes one rich,
    And He adds no sorrow with it.

Proverbs 10:21–22

Bring all the tithes into the storehouse,
That there may be food in My house,
And try Me now in this,"
Says the LORD of hosts,
"If I will not open for you the windows of heaven
And pour out for you such blessing
That there will not be room enough to receive it."

Malachi 3:10

Blessed be the LORD,
    Who daily loads us with benefits,
    The God of our salvation! Selah

Psalm 68:19

Blessed be the LORD,
    For He has shown me His marvelous kindness in a
        strong city!
For I said in my haste,
    "I am cut off from before Your eyes";
    Nevertheless You heard the voice of my supplications
    When I cried out to You.
Oh, love the LORD, all you His saints!
    For the LORD preserves the faithful,
    And fully repays the proud person.
Be of good courage,
    And He shall strengthen your heart,
    All you who hope in the LORD.

Psalm 31:21–24

For the LORD has chosen Zion;
    He has desired it for His dwelling place:
"This is My resting place forever;
    Here I will dwell, for I have desired it.
I will abundantly bless her provision;
    I will satisfy her poor with bread.
I will also clothe her priests with salvation,
    And her saints shall shout aloud for joy.

Psalm 132:13–16

A faithful man will abound with blessings,
But he who hastens to be rich will not go unpunished.

Proverbs 28:20

For when God made a promise to Abraham, because He could swear by no one greater, He swore by Himself, saying, "Surely blessing I will bless you, and multiplying I will multiply you." And so, after he had patiently endured, he obtained the promise.

Hebrews 6:13–15

I will make you a great nation;
I will bless you
And make your name great;
And you shall be a blessing.
I will bless those who bless you,
And I will curse him who curses you;
And in you all the families of the earth shall be blessed."

Genesis 12:2–3

God Promises His . . .

Compassion

But You, O Lord, are a God full of compassion, and gracious,
    Longsuffering and abundant in mercy and truth.
Oh, turn to me, and have mercy on me!
    Give Your strength to Your servant,
    And save the son of Your maidservant.

Psalm 86:15–16

But He, being full of compassion, forgave their iniquity,
    And did not destroy them.
    Yes, many a time He turned His anger away,
    And did not stir up all His wrath;
For He remembered that they were but flesh,
    A breath that passes away and does not come again.

Psalm 78:38–39

The Lord is gracious and full of compassion,
    Slow to anger and great in mercy.
The Lord is good to all,
    And His tender mercies are over all His works.

Psalm 145:8–9

Who is a God like You,
    Pardoning iniquity
    And passing over the transgression of the remnant of
His heritage?
    He does not retain His anger forever,
    Because He delights in mercy.
He will again have compassion on us,
    And will subdue our iniquities.
    You will cast all our sins
    Into the depths of the sea.

Micah 7:18–19

Your name, O LORD, endures forever,
    Your fame, O LORD, throughout all generations.
For the LORD will judge His people,
    And He will have compassion on His servants.

Psalm 135:13–14

For the Lord will not cast off forever.
Though He causes grief,
    Yet He will show compassion
    According to the multitude of His mercies.
For He does not afflict willingly,
    Nor grieve the children of men.

Lamentations 3:31–33

Then Jesus went about all the cities and villages, teaching in their synagogues, preaching the gospel of the kingdom, and healing every sickness and every disease among the people. But when He saw the multitudes, He was moved with compassion for them, because they were weary and scattered, like sheep having no shepherd. Then He said to His disciples, "The harvest truly is plentiful, but the laborers are few. Therefore pray the Lord of the harvest to send out laborers into His harvest."

Matthew 9:35–38

God Promises His . . .

Faithfulness

Your mercy, O Lord, is in the heavens;
Your faithfulness reaches to the clouds.
Your righteousness is like the great mountains;
Your judgments are a great deep;
O Lord, You preserve man and beast.
How precious is Your lovingkindness, O God!
Therefore the children of men put their trust under
the shadow of Your wings.

Psalm 36:5–7

I will sing of the mercies of the Lord forever;
With my mouth will I make known Your faithfulness to
all generations.
For I have said, "Mercy shall be built up forever;
Your faithfulness You shall establish in the very heavens."

Psalm 89:1–2

Let us draw near with a true heart in full assurance of faith, having our hearts sprinkled from an evil conscience and our bodies washed with pure water. Let us hold fast the confession of our hope without wavering, for He who promised is faithful. And let us consider one another in order to stir up love and good works.

Hebrews 10:22–24

Now may the God of peace Himself sanctify you completely; and may your whole spirit, soul, and body be preserved blameless at the coming of our Lord Jesus Christ. He who calls you is faithful, who also will do it.

1 Thessalonians 5:23–24

Forever, O Lord,
    Your word is settled in heaven.
Your faithfulness endures to all generations;
    You established the earth, and it abides.
They continue this day according to Your ordinances,
    For all are Your servants.

Psalm 119:89–91

Through the LORD's mercies we are not consumed,
    Because His compassions fail not.
They are new every morning;
    Great is Your faithfulness.
"The LORD is my portion," says my soul,
    "Therefore I hope in Him!"

Lamentations 3:22–24

No temptation has overtaken you except such as is common to man; but God is faithful, who will not allow you to be tempted beyond what you are able, but with the temptation will also make the way of escape, that you may be able to bear it.

1 Corinthians 10:13

God Promises His . . .

Kindness

Blessed be the LORD,
    For He has shown me His marvelous kindness in a
        strong city! . . .
Oh, love the LORD, all you His saints!
    For the LORD preserves the faithful,
    And fully repays the proud person.
Be of good courage,
    And He shall strengthen your heart,
    All you who hope in the LORD.

Psalm 31:21, 23–24

For the mountains shall depart
    And the hills be removed,
    But My kindness shall not depart from you,
    Nor shall My covenant of peace be removed,"
    Says the LORD, who has mercy on you.

Isaiah 54:10

But also for this very reason, giving all diligence, add to your faith virtue, to virtue knowledge, to knowledge self-control, to self-control perseverance, to perseverance godliness, to godliness brotherly kindness, and to brotherly kindness love. For if these things are yours and abound, you will be neither barren nor unfruitful in the knowledge of our Lord Jesus Christ.

2 Peter 1:5–8

Praise the LORD, all you Gentiles!
 Laud Him, all you peoples!
For His merciful kindness is great toward us,
 And the truth of the LORD endures forever.
Praise the LORD!

Psalm 117:1–2

But the fruit of the Spirit is love, joy, peace, longsuffering, kindness, goodness, faithfulness, gentleness, self-control. Against such there is no law.

Galatians 5:22–23

But when the kindness and the love of God our Savior toward man appeared, not by works of righteousness which we have done, but according to His mercy He saved us, through the washing of regeneration and renewing of the Holy Spirit.

Titus 3:4–5

But love your enemies, do good, and lend, hoping for nothing in return; and your reward will be great, and you will be sons of the Most High. For He is kind to the unthankful and evil. Therefore be merciful, just as your Father also is merciful.

Luke 6:35–36

God Promises His . . .

Patience

For whatever things were written before were written for our learning, that we through the patience and comfort of the Scriptures might have hope. Now may the God of patience and comfort grant you to be like-minded toward one another, according to Christ Jesus, that you may with one mind and one mouth glorify the God and Father of our Lord Jesus Christ.

Romans 15:4–6

My brethren, count it all joy when you fall into various trials, knowing that the testing of your faith produces patience. But let patience have its perfect work, that you may be perfect and complete, lacking nothing.

James 1:2–4

Rest in the LORD, and wait patiently for Him;
    Do not fret because of him who prospers in his way,
    Because of the man who brings wicked schemes to pass.
Cease from anger, and forsake wrath;
    Do not fret—it only causes harm.

Psalm 37:7–8

For God is not unjust to forget your work and labor of love which you have shown toward His name, in that you have ministered to the saints, and do minister. And we desire that each one of you show the same diligence to the full assurance of hope until the end, that you do not become sluggish, but imitate those who through faith and patience inherit the promises.

Hebrews 6:10–12

But you, O man of God, flee these things and pursue righteousness, godliness, faith, love, patience, gentleness. Fight the good fight of faith, lay hold on eternal life, to which you were also called and have confessed the good confession in the presence of many witnesses.

1 Timothy 6:11–12

Therefore be patient, brethren, until the coming of the Lord. See how the farmer waits for the precious fruit of the earth, waiting patiently for it until it receives the early and latter rain. You also be patient. Establish your hearts, for the coming of the Lord is at hand.

James 5:7–8

Let love be without hypocrisy. Abhor what is evil. Cling to what is good. Be kindly affectionate to one another with brotherly love, in honor giving preference to one another; not lagging in diligence, fervent in spirit, serving the Lord; rejoicing in hope, patient in tribulation, continuing steadfastly in prayer.

Romans 12:9–12

But the ones that fell on the good ground are those who, having heard the word with a noble and good heart, keep it and bear fruit with patience.

Luke 8:15

That you may walk worthy of the Lord, fully pleasing Him, being fruitful in every good work and increasing in the knowledge of God; strengthened with all might, according to His glorious power, for all patience and longsuffering with joy.

Colossians 1:10–11

We give thanks to God always for you all, making mention of you in our prayers, remembering without ceasing your work of faith, labor of love, and patience of hope in our Lord Jesus Christ in the sight of our God and Father.

1 Thessalonians 1:2–3

Now may the Lord direct your hearts into the love of God and into the patience of Christ.

2 Thessalonians 3:5

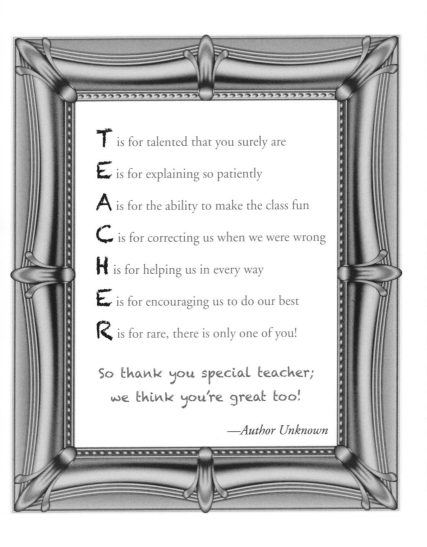

T is for talented that you surely are

E is for explaining so patiently

A is for the ability to make the class fun

C is for correcting us when we were wrong

H is for helping us in every way

E is for encouraging us to do our best

R is for rare, there is only one of you!

So thank you special teacher;
  we think you're great too!

—Author Unknown

God Promises His . . .

Forgiveness

Bless the LORD, O my soul;
    And all that is within me, bless His holy name!
Bless the LORD, O my soul,
    And forget not all His benefits:
Who forgives all your iniquities,
    Who heals all your diseases,
Who redeems your life from destruction,
    Who crowns you with lovingkindness and tender mercies.

Psalm 103:1–4

The LORD is merciful and gracious,
    Slow to anger, and abounding in mercy.
He will not always strive with us,
    Nor will He keep His anger forever.
He has not dealt with us according to our sins,
    Nor punished us according to our iniquities.
For as the heavens are high above the earth,
    So great is His mercy toward those who fear Him;
As far as the east is from the west,
    So far has He removed our transgressions from us.

Psalm 103:8–12

If we say that we have no sin, we deceive ourselves, and the truth is not in us. If we confess our sins, He is faithful and just to forgive us our sins and to cleanse us from all unrighteousness.

1 John 1:8–9

If My people who are called by My name will humble themselves, and pray and seek My face, and turn from their wicked ways, then I will hear from heaven, and will forgive their sin and heal their land.

2 Chronicles 7:14

Giving thanks to the Father who has qualified us to be partakers of the inheritance of the saints in the light. He has delivered us from the power of darkness and conveyed us into the kingdom of the Son of His love, in whom we have redemption through His blood, the forgiveness of sins.

Colossians 1:12–14

"I, even I, am He who blots out your transgressions for
   My own sake;
   And I will not remember your sins."

Isaiah 43:25

God Promises His . . .

Comfort

Blessed be the God and Father of our Lord Jesus Christ, the Father of mercies and God of all comfort, who comforts us in all our tribulation, that we may be able to comfort those who are in any trouble, with the comfort with which we ourselves are comforted by God. For as the sufferings of Christ abound in us, so our consolation also abounds through Christ.

2 Corinthians 1:3–5

Let, I pray, Your merciful kindness be for my comfort,
    According to Your word to Your servant.
Let Your tender mercies come to me, that I may live;
    For Your law is my delight.

Psalm 119:76–77

For God did not appoint us to wrath, but to obtain salvation through our Lord Jesus Christ, who died for us, that whether we wake or sleep, we should live together with Him. Therefore comfort each other and edify one another, just as you also are doing.

1 Thessalonians 5:9–11

You shall increase my greatness,
    And comfort me on every side.
Also with the lute I will praise You—
    And Your faithfulness, O my God!
    To You I will sing with the harp,
    O Holy One of Israel.
My lips shall greatly rejoice when I sing to You,
    And my soul, which You have redeemed.

Psalm 71:21–23

For the Lord will comfort Zion,
    He will comfort all her waste places;
    He will make her wilderness like Eden,
    And her desert like the garden of the Lord;
Joy and gladness will be found in it,
    Thanksgiving and the voice of melody.

Isaiah 51:3

Unless the Lord had been my help,
    My soul would soon have settled in silence.
If I say, "My foot slips,"
    Your mercy, O Lord, will hold me up.
In the multitude of my anxieties within me,
    Your comforts delight my soul.

Psalm 94:17–19

God Promises His . . .

Power

Have you not known?
  Have you not heard?
  The everlasting God, the Lord,
  The Creator of the ends of the earth,
  Neither faints nor is weary.
  His understanding is unsearchable.
He gives power to the weak,
  And to those who have no might He increases strength.
Even the youths shall faint and be weary,
  And the young men shall utterly fall,
But those who wait on the Lord
  Shall renew their strength;
  They shall mount up with wings like eagles,
  They shall run and not be weary,
  They shall walk and not faint.

Isaiah 40:28–31

Believe Me that I am in the Father and the Father in Me, or else believe Me for the sake of the works themselves. "Most assuredly, I say to you, he who believes in Me, the works that I do he will do also; and greater works than these he will do, because I go to My Father. And whatever you ask in My name, that I will do, that the Father may be glorified in the Son."

John 14:11–13

God has spoken once,
 Twice I have heard this:
 That power belongs to God.
Also to You, O LORD, belongs mercy;
 For You render to each one according to his work.

Psalm 62:11–12

Ascribe strength to God;
 His excellence is over Israel,
 And His strength is in the clouds.
O God, You are more awesome than Your holy places.
 The God of Israel is He who gives strength and power
to His people.
 Blessed be God!

Psalm 68:34–35

For I determined not to know anything among you except Jesus Christ and Him crucified. I was with you in weakness, in fear, and in much trembling. And my speech and my preaching were not with persuasive words of human wisdom, but in demonstration of the Spirit and of power, that your faith should not be in the wisdom of men but in the power of God.

1 Corinthians 2:2–5

And He said to me, "My grace is sufficient for you, for My strength is made perfect in weakness." Therefore most gladly I will rather boast in my infirmities, that the power of Christ may rest upon me. Therefore I take pleasure in infirmities, in reproaches, in needs, in persecutions, in distresses, for Christ's sake. For when I am weak, then I am strong.

2 Corinthians 12:9–10

God Promises His . . .

Strength

I can do all things through Christ who strengthens me.

Philippians 4:13

The LORD is my strength and my shield;
    My heart trusted in Him, and I am helped;
    Therefore my heart greatly rejoices,
    And with my song I will praise Him.
The LORD is their strength,
    And He is the saving refuge of His anointed.
Save Your people,
    And bless Your inheritance;
    Shepherd them also,
    And bear them up forever.

Psalm 28:7–9

In that day this song will be sung in the land of Judah:
    "We have a strong city;
    God will appoint salvation for walls and bulwarks."

Isaiah 26:1

Give unto the LORD, O you mighty ones,
  Give unto the LORD glory and strength.
Give unto the LORD the glory due to His name;
  Worship the LORD in the beauty of holiness.
The voice of the LORD is over the waters;
  The God of glory thunders;
  The Lord is over many waters.
The voice of the LORD is powerful;
  The voice of the LORD is full of majesty. . . .
The voice of the LORD makes the deer give birth,
  And strips the forests bare;
  And in His temple everyone says, "Glory!"
The LORD sat enthroned at the Flood,
  And the LORD sits as King forever.
The LORD will give strength to His people;
  The LORD will bless His people with peace.

Psalm 29:1–4, 9–11

"Fear not, for I am with you;
  Be not dismayed, for I am your God.
  I will strengthen you,
  Yes, I will help you,
  I will uphold you with My righteous right hand."

Isaiah 41:10

God is our refuge and strength,
   A very present help in trouble.
Therefore we will not fear,
   Even though the earth be removed,
   And though the mountains be carried into the midst
      of the sea;
Though its waters roar and be troubled,
   Though the mountains shake with its swelling. Selah
There is a river whose streams shall make glad the city of God,
   The holy place of the tabernacle of the Most High.
God is in the midst of her, she shall not be moved;
   God shall help her, just at the break of dawn.

Psalm 46:1–5

God Promises His . . .

Presence

I know that the LORD will maintain
    The cause of the afflicted,
    And justice for the poor.
Surely the righteous shall give thanks to Your name;
    The upright shall dwell in Your presence.

Psalm 140:12–13

For Christ has not entered the holy places made with hands, which are copies of the true, but into heaven itself, now to appear in the presence of God for us.

Hebrews 9:24

I have set the LORD always before me;
    Because He is at my right hand I shall not be moved.
Therefore my heart is glad, and my glory rejoices;
    My flesh also will rest in hope. . . .
You will show me the path of life;
    In Your presence is fullness of joy;
    At Your right hand are pleasures forevermore.

Psalm 16:8–9, 11

Those who trust in the LORD
  Are like Mount Zion,
    Which cannot be moved, but abides forever.
As the mountains surround Jerusalem,
  So the LORD surrounds His people
  From this time forth and forever.

Psalm 125:1–2

So then, those who are in the flesh cannot please God. But you are not in the flesh but in the Spirit, if indeed the Spirit of God dwells in you. Now if anyone does not have the Spirit of Christ, he is not His.

Romans 8:8–9

I will give you a new heart and put a new spirit within you; I will take the heart of stone out of your flesh and give you a heart of flesh. I will put My Spirit within you and cause you to walk in My statutes, and you will keep My judgments and do them. Then you shall dwell in the land that I gave to your fathers; you shall be My people, and I will be your God.

Ezekiel 36:26–28

Be strong and of good courage, do not fear nor be afraid of them; for the Lord your God, He is the One who goes with you. He will not leave you nor forsake you.

Deuteronomy 31:6

God Promises His . . .

Peace

These things I have spoken to you, that in Me you may have peace. In the world you will have tribulation; but be of good cheer, I have overcome the world.

John 16:33

And let the peace of God rule in your hearts, to which also you were called in one body; and be thankful.

Colossians 3:15

Peace I leave with you, My peace I give to you; not as the world gives do I give to you. Let not your heart be troubled, neither let it be afraid. You have heard Me say to you, "I am going away and coming back to you." If you loved Me, you would rejoice because I said, "I am going to the Father," for My Father is greater than I.

John 14:27–28

Finally, brethren, farewell. Become complete. Be of good comfort, be of one mind, live in peace; and the God of love and peace will be with you.

2 Corinthians 13:11

You will keep him in perfect peace,
    Whose mind is stayed on You,
    Because he trusts in You.
    Trust in the Lord forever,
    For in YAH, the LORD, is everlasting strength.

Isaiah 26:3–4

For He Himself is our peace, who has made both one, and has broken down the middle wall of separation, having abolished in His flesh the enmity, that is, the law of commandments contained in ordinances, so as to create in Himself one new man from the two, thus making peace.

Ephesians 2:14–15

God Promises His . . .

Guidance

Commit your works to the LORD,
And your thoughts will be established.

Proverbs 16:3

The LORD will guide you continually,
 And satisfy your soul in drought,
 And strengthen your bones;
 You shall be like a watered garden,
 And like a spring of water, whose waters do not fail.

Isaiah 58:11

Thus says the Lord, your Redeemer,
 The Holy One of Israel:
 "I am the LORD your God,
 Who teaches you to profit,
 Who leads you by the way you should go."

Isaiah 48:17

I will put My Spirit within you and cause you to walk in My statutes, and you will keep My judgments and do them.

Ezekiel 36:27

However, when He, the Spirit of truth, has come, He will guide you into all truth; for He will not speak on His own authority, but whatever He hears He will speak; and He will tell you things to come.

John 16:13

For this is God,
    Our God forever and ever;
    He will be our guide
    Even to death.

Psalm 48:14

I will instruct you and teach you in the way you should go;
    I will guide you with My eye.

Psalm 32:8

This also comes from the LORD of hosts,
    Who is wonderful in counsel and excellent in guidance.

Isaiah 28:29

God's Promises His . . .

Wisdom

Abide in Me, and I in you. As the branch cannot bear fruit of itself, unless it abides in the vine, neither can you, unless you abide in Me. "I am the vine, you are the branches. He who abides in Me, and I in him, bears much fruit; for without Me you can do nothing. If anyone does not abide in Me, he is cast out as a branch and is withered; and they gather them and throw them into the fire, and they are burned. If you abide in Me, and My words abide in you, you will ask what you desire, and it shall be done for you.

John 15:4–7

Get wisdom! Get understanding!
 Do not forget, nor turn away from the words of my mouth.
  Do not forsake her, and she will preserve you;
 Love her, and she will keep you.
  Wisdom is the principal thing;
 Therefore get wisdom.
 And in all your getting, get understanding.
  Exalt her, and she will promote you;
 She will bring you honor, when you embrace her.

Proverbs 4:5–8

My son, if you receive my words,
    And treasure my commands within you,
So that you incline your ear to wisdom,
    And apply your heart to understanding;
Yes, if you cry out for discernment,
    And lift up your voice for understanding,
If you seek her as silver,
    And search for her as for hidden treasures;
Then you will understand the fear of the LORD,
    And find the knowledge of God.
For the LORD gives wisdom;
    From His mouth come knowledge and understanding;
He stores up sound wisdom for the upright;
    He is a shield to those who walk uprightly.

Proverbs 2:1–7

Happy is the man who finds wisdom,
    And the man who gains understanding;
For her proceeds are better than the profits of silver,
    And her gain than fine gold.
She is more precious than rubies,
    And all the things you may desire cannot compare with her.
Length of days is in her right hand,
    In her left hand riches and honor.
Her ways are ways of pleasantness,
    And all her paths are peace.
She is a tree of life to those who take hold of her,
    And happy are all who retain her.

Proverbs 3:13–18

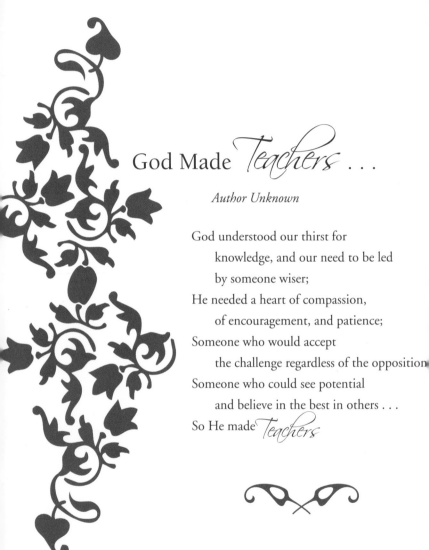

God Made *Teachers* . . .

Author Unknown

God understood our thirst for
knowledge, and our need to be led
by someone wiser;
He needed a heart of compassion,
of encouragement, and patience;
Someone who would accept
the challenge regardless of the opposition
Someone who could see potential
and believe in the best in others . . .
So He made *Teachers*

God Promises His . . .

Eternal Gift

"Most assuredly, I say to you, he who hears My word and believes in Him who sent Me has everlasting life, and shall not come into judgment, but has passed from death into life. Most assuredly, I say to you, the hour is coming, and now is, when the dead will hear the voice of the Son of God; and those who hear will live. For as the Father has life in Himself, so He has granted the Son to have life in Himself."

John 5:24–26

My sheep hear My voice, and I know them, and they follow Me. And I give them eternal life, and they shall never perish; neither shall anyone snatch them out of My hand. My Father, who has given them to Me, is greater than all; and no one is able to snatch them out of My Father's hand.

John 10:27–29

No one has ascended to heaven but He who came down from heaven, that is, the Son of Man who is in heaven. . . . that whoever believes in Him should not perish but have eternal life. For God so loved the world that He gave His only begotten Son, that whoever believes in Him should not perish but have everlasting life.

John 3:13, 15–16

But now having been set free from sin, and having become slaves of God, you have your fruit to holiness, and the end, everlasting life. For the wages of sin is death, but the gift of God is eternal life in Christ Jesus our Lord.

Romans 6:22–23

This is a faithful saying and worthy of all acceptance, that Christ Jesus came into the world to save sinners, of whom I am chief. However, for this reason I obtained mercy, that in me first Jesus Christ might show all longsuffering, as a pattern to those who are going to believe on Him for everlasting life. Now to the King eternal, immortal, invisible, to God who alone is wise, be honor and glory forever and ever. Amen.

1 Timothy 1:15–17

Do not be deceived, God is not mocked; for whatever a man sows, that he will also reap. For he who sows to his flesh will of the flesh reap corruption, but he who sows to the Spirit will of the Spirit reap everlasting life.

Galatians 6:7–8

Jesus answered and said to her, "Whoever drinks of this water will thirst again, but whoever drinks of the water that I shall give him will never thirst. But the water that I shall give him will become in him a fountain of water springing up into everlasting life."

John 4:13–14

God Promises His . . .

Goodness

Yea, though I walk through the valley of the shadow of death,
  I will fear no evil;
  For You are with me;
  Your rod and Your staff, they comfort me.
You prepare a table before me in the presence of my enemies;
  You anoint my head with oil;
  My cup runs over.
Surely goodness and mercy shall follow me
  All the days of my life;
  And I will dwell in the house of the Lord
  Forever.

Psalm 23:4–6

Teach me Your way, O Lord,
  And lead me in a smooth path, because of my enemies.
Do not deliver me to the will of my adversaries;
  For false witnesses have risen against me,
  And such as breathe out violence.
I would have lost heart, unless I had believed
  That I would see the goodness of the Lord
  In the land of the living.

Wait on the LORD;
    Be of good courage,
    And He shall strengthen your heart;
    Wait, I say, on the LORD!

Psalm 27:11–14

Oh, how great is Your goodness,
    Which You have laid up for those who fear You,
    Which You have prepared for those who trust in You
    In the presence of the sons of men!
You shall hide them in the secret place of Your presence
    From the plots of man;
    You shall keep them secretly in a pavilion
    From the strife of tongues.
Blessed be the LORD,
    For He has shown me His marvelous kindness in a
       strong city!

Psalm 31:19–21

But we know that the judgment of God is according to truth against those who practice such things. And do you think this, O man, you who judge those practicing such things, and doing the same, that you will escape the judgment of God? Or do you despise the riches of His goodness, forbearance, and longsuffering, not knowing that the goodness of God leads you to repentance?

Romans 2:2–4

Now the LORD descended in the cloud and stood with him there, and proclaimed the name of the LORD. And the LORD passed before him and proclaimed, "The LORD, the LORD God, merciful and gracious, longsuffering, and abounding in goodness and truth."

Exodus 34:5–6

Why do you boast in evil, O mighty man?
 The goodness of God endures continually.

Psalm 52:1

Do not boast against the branches. But if you do boast, remember that you do not support the root, but the root supports you.

You will say then, "Branches were broken off that I might be grafted in." Well said. Because of unbelief they were broken off, and you stand by faith. Do not be haughty, but fear. For if God did not spare the natural branches, He may not spare you either. Therefore consider the goodness and severity of God: on those who fell, severity; but toward you, goodness, if you continue in His goodness. Otherwise you also will be cut off.

Romans 11:18–22

But the fruit of the Spirit is love, joy, peace, longsuffering, kindness, goodness, faithfulness.

Galatians 5:22

God Promises His . . .

Favor

Blessed is the man who listens to me,
  Watching daily at my gates,
  Waiting at the posts of my doors.
For whoever finds me finds life,
  And obtains favor from the LORD.

Proverbs 8:34–35

The law of the wise is a fountain of life,
  To turn one away from the snares of death.
Good understanding gains favor,
  But the way of the unfaithful is hard.

Proverbs 13:14–15

The king's wrath is like the roaring of a lion,
  But his favor is like dew on the grass.

Proverbs 19:12

Sing praise to the Lord, you saints of His,
    And give thanks at the remembrance of His holy name.
For His anger is but for a moment,
    His favor is for life;
    Weeping may endure for a night,
    But joy comes in the morning.

Psalm 30:4–5

But let all those rejoice who put their trust in You;
    Let them ever shout for joy, because You defend them;
    Let those also who love Your name
    Be joyful in You.
For You, O Lord, will bless the righteous;
    With favor You will surround him as with a shield.

Psalm 5:11–12

Enter into His gates with thanksgiving,
    And into His courts with praise.
    Be thankful to Him, and bless His name.
For the Lord is good;
    His mercy is everlasting,
    And His truth endures to all generations.

Psalm 100:4–5

Let them shout for joy and be glad,
   Who favor y righteous cause;
   And let them say continually,
   "Let the Lord be magnified,
   Who has pleasure in the prosperity of His servant."
And my tongue shall speak of Your righteousness
   And of Your praise all the day long.

Psalm 35:27–28

Bless My *Teacher*

Dear Jesus,

Bless every teacher with the Light of Your love, a heavenly vision, a gift from above. May they catch a glimpse of lives yet untold, bring hope for tomorrow in each child to unfold. May they shine like a star, reflecting your glory. May they be a chapter in each child's lifelong story. Amen.

—Karla Dornacher

God Promises His . . .

Heaven

"Behold, I give you the authority to trample on serpents and scorpions, and over all the power of the enemy, and nothing shall by any means hurt you. Nevertheless do not rejoice in this, that the spirits are subject to you, but rather rejoice because your names are written in heaven." In that hour Jesus rejoiced in the Spirit and said, "I thank You, Father, Lord of heaven and earth, that You have hidden these things from the wise and prudent and revealed them to babes. Even so, Father, for so it seemed good in Your sight."

Luke 10:19–21

Since we heard of your faith in Christ Jesus and of your love for all the saints; because of the hope which is laid up for you in heaven, of which you heard before in the word of the truth of the gospel, which has come to you, as it has also in all the world, and is bringing forth fruit, as it is also among you since the day you heard and knew the grace of God in truth.

Colossians 1:4–6

I say to you that likewise there will be more joy in heaven over one sinner who repents than over ninety-nine just persons who need no repentance.

Luke 15:7

I will lift up my eyes to the hills—
　　From whence comes my help?
My help comes from the LORD,
　　Who made heaven and earth.
He will not allow your foot to be moved;
　　He who keeps you will not slumber.

Psalm 121:1–3

Thus says the LORD:
　　"Heaven is My throne,
　　And earth is My footstool.
　　Where is the house that you will build Me?
　　And where is the place of My rest?
For all those things My hand has made,
　　And all those things exist,"
　　Says the LORD.
　　"But on this one will I look:
　　On him who is poor and of a contrite spirit,
　　And who trembles at My word."

Isaiah 66:1–2

Now I saw a new heaven and a new earth, for the first heaven and the first earth had passed away. Also there was no more sea. Then I, John, saw the holy city, New Jerusalem, coming down out of heaven from God, prepared as a bride adorned for her husband. And I heard a loud voice from heaven saying, "Behold, the tabernacle of God is with men, and He will dwell with them, and they shall be His people. God Himself will be with them and be their God. And God will wipe away every tear from their eyes; there shall be no more death, nor sorrow, nor crying. There shall be no more pain, for the former things have passed away."

Revelation 21:1–4

Then Jesus said to them, "Most assuredly, I say to you, Moses did not give you the bread from heaven, but My Father gives you the true bread from heaven. For the bread of God is He who comes down from heaven and gives life to the world."

Then they said to Him, "Lord, give us this bread always."

And Jesus said to them, "I am the bread of life. He who comes to Me shall never hunger, and he who believes in Me shall never thirst. But I said to you that you have seen Me and yet do not believe. All that the Father gives Me will come to Me, and the one who comes to Me I will by no means cast out. For I have come down from heaven, not to do My own will, but the will of Him who sent Me. This is the will of the Father who sent Me, that of all He has given Me I should lose nothing, but should raise it up at the last day."

John 6:32–39

God Promises His . . .

Angels

The angel of the LORD encamps all around those who
	fear Him,
	And delivers them.
Oh, taste and see that the LORD is good;
	Blessed is the man who trusts in Him!
Oh, fear the LORD, you His saints!
	There is no want to those who fear Him.
The young lions lack and suffer hunger;
	But those who seek the LORD shall not lack any good thing.
Psalm 34:7–10

Then I saw a strong angel proclaiming with a loud voice, "Who
is worthy to open the scroll and to loose its seals?" And no one in
heaven or on the earth or under the earth was able to open the
scroll, or to look at it.

So I wept much, because no one was found worthy to open and
read the scroll, or to look at it. But one of the elders said to me,
"Do not weep. Behold, the Lion of the tribe of Judah, the Root of
David, has prevailed to open the scroll and to loose its seven seals."
Revelation 5:2–5

And behold, there was a great earthquake; for an angel of the Lord descended from heaven, and came and rolled back the stone from the door, and sat on it. His countenance was like lightning, and his clothing as white as snow. And the guards shook for fear of him, and became like dead men.

But the angel answered and said to the women, "Do not be afraid, for I know that you seek Jesus who was crucified. He is not here; for He is risen, as He said. Come, see the place where the Lord lay. And go quickly and tell His disciples that He is risen from the dead, and indeed He is going before you into Galilee; there you will see Him. Behold, I have told you."

Matthew 28:2–7

No evil shall befall you,
    Nor shall any plague come near your dwelling;
For He shall give His angels charge over you,
    To keep you in all your ways.
In their hands they shall bear you up,
    Lest you dash your foot against a stone.
You shall tread upon the lion and the cobra,
    The young lion and the serpent you shall trample underfoot.
"Because he has set his love upon Me, therefore I will deliver him;
    I will set him on high, because he has known My name.
He shall call upon Me, and I will answer him;
    I will be with him in trouble;
    I will deliver him and honor him.
With long life I will satisfy him,
    And show him My salvation."

Psalm 91:10–16

Praise Him, all His angels;
    Praise Him, all His hosts!
Praise Him, sun and moon;
    Praise Him, all you stars of light!
Praise Him, you heavens of heavens,
    And you waters above the heavens!
Let them praise the name of the LORD,
    For He commanded and they were created.
He also established them forever and ever;
    He made a decree which shall not pass away.

Psalm 148:2–6

Then the Angel of the LORD called to Abraham a second time out of heaven, and said: "By Myself I have sworn, says the LORD, because you have done this thing, and have not withheld your son, your only son—blessing I will bless you, and multiplying I will multiply your descendants as the stars of the heaven and as the sand which is on the seashore; and your descendants shall possess the gate of their enemies. In your seed all the nations of the earth shall be blessed, because you have obeyed My voice." So Abraham returned to his young men, and they rose and went together to Beersheba; and Abraham dwelt at Beersheba.

Genesis 22:15–19

God Promises His . . .

Light

Then Jesus spoke to them again, saying, "I am the light of the world. He who follows Me shall not walk in darkness, but have the light of life."

John 8:12

Therefore take heed that the light which is in you is not darkness. If then your whole body is full of light, having no part dark, the whole body will be full of light, as when the bright shining of a lamp gives you light."

Luke 11:35–36

This is the message which we have heard from Him and declare to you, that God is light and in Him is no darkness at all. If we say that we have fellowship with Him, and walk in darkness, we lie and do not practice the truth. But if we walk in the light as He is in the light, we have fellowship with one another, and the blood of Jesus Christ His Son cleanses us from all sin.

1 John 1:5–7

In the beginning was the Word, and the Word was with God, and the Word was God. He was in the beginning with God. All things were made through Him, and without Him nothing was made that was made. In Him was life, and the life was the light of men. And the light shines in the darkness, and the darkness did not comprehend it.

There was a man sent from God, whose name was John. This man came for a witness, to bear witness of the Light, that all through him might believe. He was not that Light, but was sent to bear witness of that Light. That was the true Light which gives light to every man coming into the world.

John 1:1–9

The LORD is my light and my salvation;
    Whom shall I fear?
    The LORD is the strength of my life;
    Of whom shall I be afraid?
When the wicked came against me
    To eat up my flesh,
    My enemies and foes,
    They stumbled and fell.
Though an army may encamp against me,
    My heart shall not fear;
    Though war may rise against me,
    In this I will be confident.

Psalm 27:1–3

Then Jesus said to them, "A little while longer the light is with you. Walk while you have the light, lest darkness overtake you; he who walks in darkness does not know where he is going. While you have the light, believe in the light, that you may become sons of light." These things Jesus spoke, and departed, and was hidden from them.

But although He had done so many signs before them, they did not believe in Him, . . .

And he who sees Me sees Him who sent Me. I have come as a light into the world, that whoever believes in Me should not abide in darkness.

John 12:35–37, 45–46

"You are the light of the world. A city that is set on a hill cannot be hidden. Nor do they light a lamp and put it under a basket, but on a lampstand, and it gives light to all who are in the house. Let your light so shine before men, that they may see your good works and glorify your Father in heaven."

Matthew 5:14–16

God Promises His . . .

Sacrifice

Be silent in the presence of the LORD GOD;
    For the day of the LORD is at hand,
    For the LORD has prepared a sacrifice;
    He has invited His guests.
"And it shall be,
    In the day of the LORD's sacrifice,
    That I will punish the princes and the king's children,
    And all such as are clothed with foreign apparel."

Zephaniah 1:7–8

I beseech you therefore, brethren, by the mercies of God, that you present your bodies a living sacrifice, holy, acceptable to God, which is your reasonable service. And do not be conformed to this world, but be transformed by the renewing of your mind, that you may prove what is that good and acceptable and perfect will of God.

Romans 12:1–2

Therefore be imitators of God as dear children. And walk in love, as Christ also has loved us and given Himself for us, an offering and a sacrifice to God for a sweet-smelling aroma.

Ephesians 5:1–2

For Christ has not entered the holy places made with hands, which are copies of the true, but into heaven itself, now to appear in the presence of God for us; not that He should offer Himself often, as the high priest enters the Most Holy Place every year with blood of another—He then would have had to suffer often since the foundation of the world; but now, once at the end of the ages, He has appeared to put away sin by the sacrifice of Himself.

Hebrews 9:24–26

Then He said, "Behold, I have come to do Your will, O God." He takes away the first that He may establish the second. By that will we have been sanctified through the offering of the body of Jesus Christ once for all.

And every priest stands ministering daily and offering repeatedly the same sacrifices, which can never take away sins. But this Man, after He had offered one sacrifice for sins forever, sat down at the right hand of God.

Hebrews 10:9–12

You also, as living stones, are being built up a spiritual house, a holy priesthood, to offer up spiritual sacrifices acceptable to God through Jesus Christ. Therefore it is also contained in the Scripture,

> "Behold, I lay in Zion
> A chief cornerstone, elect, precious,
> And he who believes on Him will by no means be put
>   to shame."

1 Peter 2:5–6

Therefore by Him let us continually offer the sacrifice of praise to God, that is, the fruit of our lips, giving thanks to His name. But do not forget to do good and to share, for with such sacrifices God is well pleased.

Hebrews 13:15–16

God Promises His . . .

Covenant

"Now therefore, if you will indeed obey My voice and keep My covenant, then you shall be a special treasure to Me above all people; for all the earth is Mine. And you shall be to Me a kingdom of priests and a holy nation.' These are the words which you shall speak to the children of Israel."

So Moses came and called for the elders of the people, and laid before them all these words which the LORD commanded him. Then all the people answered together and said, "All that the LORD has spoken we will do." So Moses brought back the words of the people to the LORD.

Exodus 19:5–8

Now may the God of peace who brought up our LORD Jesus from the dead, that great Shepherd of the sheep, through the blood of the everlasting covenant, make you complete in every good work to do His will, working in you what is well pleasing in His sight, through Jesus Christ, to whom be glory forever and ever. Amen.

Hebrews 13:20–21

To Jesus the Mediator of the new covenant, and to the blood of sprinkling that speaks better things than that of Abel.

See that you do not refuse Him who speaks. For if they did not escape who refused Him who spoke on earth, much more shall we not escape if we turn away from Him who speaks from heaven, whose voice then shook the earth; but now He has promised, saying, "Yet once more I shake not only the earth, but also heaven." Now this, "Yet once more," indicates the removal of those things that are being shaken, as of things that are made, that the things which cannot be shaken may remain.

Therefore, since we are receiving a kingdom which cannot be shaken, let us have grace, by which we may serve God acceptably with reverence and godly fear.

Hebrews 12:24–28

And it came to pass, when the sun went down and it was dark, that behold, there appeared a smoking oven and a burning torch that passed between those pieces. On the same day the LORD made a covenant with Abram, saying:

"To your descendants I have given this land, from the river of Egypt to the great river, the River Euphrates—the Kenites, the Kenezzites, the Kadmonites, the Hittites, the Perizzites, the Rephaim, the Amorites, the Canaanites, the Girgashites, and the Jebusites."

Genesis 15:17–21

"Behold, I send My messenger,
    And he will prepare the way before Me.
    And the LORD, whom you seek,
    Will suddenly come to His temple,
    Even the Messenger of the covenant,
    In whom you delight.
    Behold, He is coming,"
    Says the LORD of hosts.
"But who can endure the day of His coming?
    And who can stand when He appears?
    For He is like a refiner's fire
    And like launderers' soap.
He will sit as a refiner and a purifier of silver;
    He will purify the sons of Levi,
    And purge them as gold and silver,
    That they may offer to the LORD
    An offering in righteousness.

Malachi 3:1–3

But this is the covenant that I will make with the house of Israel after those days, says the LORD: I will put My law in their minds, and write it on their hearts; and I will be their God, and they shall be My people.

Jeremiah 31:33

But now He has obtained a more excellent ministry, inasmuch as He is also Mediator of a better covenant, which was established on better promises.

For if that first covenant had been faultless, then no place would have been sought for a second. Because finding fault with them, He says: "Behold, the days are coming, says the LORD, when I will make a new covenant with the house of Israel and with the house of Judah—not according to the covenant that I made with their fathers in the day when I took them by the hand to lead them out of the land of Egypt; because they did not continue in My covenant, and I disregarded them, says the LORD. For this is the covenant that I will make with the house of Israel after those days, says the LORD: I will put My laws in their mind and write them on their hearts; and I will be their God, and they shall be My people.

Hebrews 8:6–10

God Promises His . . .

Holiness

Therefore, having these promises, beloved, let us cleanse ourselves from all filthiness of the flesh and spirit, perfecting holiness in the fear of God.

2 Corinthians 7:1

For God did not call us to uncleanness, but in holiness. Therefore he who rejects this does not reject man, but God, who has also given us His Holy Spirit.

1 Thessalonians 4:7–8

A highway shall be there, and a road,
   And it shall be called the Highway of Holiness.
   The unclean shall not pass over it,
   But it shall be for others.
   Whoever walks the road, although a fool,
   Shall not go astray.

Isaiah 35:8

Paul, a bondservant of Jesus Christ, called to be an apostle, separated to the gospel of God which He promised before through His prophets in the Holy Scriptures, concerning His Son Jesus Christ our Lord, who was born of the seed of David according to the flesh, and declared to be the Son of God with power according to the Spirit of holiness, by the resurrection from the dead. Through Him we have received grace and apostleship for obedience to the faith among all nations for His name, among whom you also are the called of Jesus Christ.

Romans 1:1–6

"Who is like You, O LORD, among the gods?
    Who is like You, glorious in holiness,
    Fearful in praises, doing wonders?
You stretched out Your right hand;
    The earth swallowed them.
You in Your mercy have led forth
    The people whom You have redeemed;
    You have guided them in Your strength
    To Your holy habitation."

Exodus 15:11–13

Give to the LORD, O families of the peoples,
  Give to the LORD glory and strength.
Give to the LORD the glory due His name;
  Bring an offering, and come before Him.
  Oh, worship the LORD in the beauty of holiness!

1 Chronicles 16:28–29

Nevertheless My lovingkindness I will not utterly take
    from him,
  Nor allow My faithfulness to fail.
My covenant I will not break,
  Nor alter the word that has gone out of My lips.
Once I have sworn by My holiness;
  I will not lie to David:
His seed shall endure forever,
  And his throne as the sun before Me;
It shall be established forever like the moon,
  Even like the faithful witness in the sky." Selah

Psalm 89:33–37

God Promises His . . .

Spirit

So then, those who are in the flesh cannot please God.

But you are not in the flesh but in the Spirit, if indeed the Spirit of God dwells in you. Now if anyone does not have the Spirit of Christ, he is not His. And if Christ is in you, the body is dead because of sin, but the Spirit is life because of righteousness. But if the Spirit of Him who raised Jesus from the dead dwells in you, He who raised Christ from the dead will also give life to your mortal bodies through His Spirit who dwells in you.

Romans 8:8–11

Nevertheless when one turns to the Lord, the veil is taken away. Now the Lord is the Spirit; and where the Spirit of the Lord is, there is liberty. But we all, with unveiled face, beholding as in a mirror the glory of the Lord, are being transformed into the same image from glory to glory, just as by the Spirit of the Lord.

2 Corinthians 3:16–18

But as it is written:

"Eye has not seen, nor ear heard,
Nor have entered into the heart of man
The things which God has prepared for those who
    love Him."

But God has revealed them to us through His Spirit. For the Spirit searches all things, yes, the deep things of God. For what man knows the things of a man except the spirit of the man which is in him? Even so no one knows the things of God except the Spirit of God. Now we have received, not the spirit of the world, but the Spirit who is from God, that we might know the things that have been freely given to us by God.

1 Corinthians 2:9–12

Beloved, do not believe every spirit, but test the spirits, whether they are of God; because many false prophets have gone out into the world. By this you know the Spirit of God: Every spirit that confesses that Jesus Christ has come in the flesh is of God, and every spirit that does not confess that Jesus Christ has come in the flesh is not of God. And this is the spirit of the Antichrist, which you have heard was coming, and is now already in the world.

1 John 4:1–3

Do you not know that you are the temple of God and that the Spirit of God dwells in you? If anyone defiles the temple of God, God will destroy him. For the temple of God is holy, which temple you are.

1 Corinthians 3:16–17

When He had been baptized, Jesus came up immediately from the water; and behold, the heavens were opened to Him, and He saw the Spirit of God descending like a dove and alighting upon Him. And suddenly a voice came from heaven, saying, "This is My beloved Son, in whom I am well pleased."

Matthew 3:16–17

God Promises His . . .

Encouragement

Who is this King of glory?
    The LORD strong and mighty,
    The LORD mighty in battle.
Lift up your heads, O you gates!
    Lift up, you everlasting doors!
    And the King of glory shall come in.

Psalm 24:8–9

Because Your lovingkindness is better than life,
    My lips shall praise You.
Thus I will bless You while I live;
    I will lift up my hands in Your name.
My soul shall be satisfied as with marrow and fatness,
    And my mouth shall praise You with joyful lips.

Psalm 63:3–5

The LORD is your keeper;
    The LORD is your shade at your right hand.
The sun shall not strike you by day,
    Nor the moon by night. . . .
The LORD shall preserve your going out and your coming in
    From this time forth, and even forevermore.

Psalm 121:5–6, 8

For I want you to know what a great conflict I have for you and those in Laodicea, and for as many as have not seen my face in the flesh, that their hearts may be encouraged, being knit together in love, and attaining to all riches of the full assurance of understanding, to the knowledge of the mystery of God, both of the Father and of Christ, in whom are hidden all the treasures of wisdom and knowledge.

Colossians 2:1–3

Humble yourselves in the sight of the Lord, and He will lift you up.

Do not speak evil of one another, brethren. He who speaks evil of a brother and judges his brother, speaks evil of the law and judges the law. But if you judge the law, you are not a doer of the law but a judge.

James 4:10–11

Whose Child
Is This?

Author Unknown

"Whose child is this?" I asked one day
    Seeing a little one out at play
"Mine," said the parent with a tender smile
"Mine to keep a little while
    To bathe his hands and comb his hair
    To tell him what he is to wear
    To prepare him that he may always be good
    And each day do the things he should."

"Whose child is this?" I asked again
    As the door opened and someone came in
"Mine," said the teacher with the same
    tender smile
"Mine, to keep just for a little while
    To teach him how to be gentle and kind
    To train and direct his dear little mind
    To help him live by every rule
    And get the best he can from school."

"Whose child is this?" I asked once more
    Just as the little one entered the door
"Ours" said the parent and the teacher as
            they smiled
    And each took the hand of the little child
"Ours to love and train together
    Ours this blessed task forever."

God
Promises Your . . .

God Promises Your . . .

Salvation

If you confess with your mouth the Lord Jesus and believe in your heart that God has raised Him from the dead, you will be saved. For with the heart one believes unto righteousness, and with the mouth confession is made unto salvation. For the Scripture says, "Whoever believes on Him will not be put to shame." For there is no distinction between Jew and Greek, for the same Lord over all is rich to all who call upon Him. For "whoever calls on the name of the LORD shall be saved."

Romans 10:9–13

But we are bound to give thanks to God always for you, brethren beloved by the Lord, because God from the beginning chose you for salvation through sanctification by the Spirit and belief in the truth, to which He called you by our gospel, for the obtaining of the glory of our Lord Jesus Christ.

2 Thessalonians 2:13–14

For by grace you have been saved through faith, and that not of yourselves; it is the gift of God, not of works, lest anyone should boast. For we are His workmanship, created in Christ Jesus for good works, which God prepared beforehand that we should walk in them.

Ephesians 2:8–10

For God so loved the world that He gave His only begotten Son, that whoever believes in Him should not perish but have everlasting life. For God did not send His Son into the world to condemn the world, but that the world through Him might be saved.

John 3:16–17

Therefore, my beloved, as you have always obeyed, not as in my presence only, but now much more in my absence, work out your own salvation with fear and trembling; for it is God who works in you both to will and to do for His good pleasure.

Philippians 2:12–13

For I am not ashamed of the gospel of Christ, for it is the power of God to salvation for everyone who believes, for the Jew first and also for the Greek. For in it the righteousness of God is revealed from faith to faith; as it is written, "The just shall live by faith."

Romans 1:16–17

God Promises Your . . .

Inheritance

O Lord, You are the portion of my inheritance and my cup;
    You maintain my lot.
The lines have fallen to me in pleasant places;
    Yes, I have a good inheritance.
I will bless the Lord who has given me counsel;
    My heart also instructs me in the night seasons.

Psalm 16:5–7

The Lord knows the days of the upright,
    And their inheritance shall be forever.
They shall not be ashamed in the evil time,
    And in the days of famine they shall be satisfied.

Psalm 37:18–19

In Him also we have obtained an inheritance, being predestined according to the purpose of Him who works all things according to the counsel of His will, that we who first trusted in Christ should be to the praise of His glory.

Ephesians 1:11–12

Oh, clap your hands, all you peoples!
    Shout to God with the voice of triumph!
For the LORD Most High is awesome;
    He is a great King over all the earth.
He will subdue the peoples under us,
    And the nations under our feet.
He will choose our inheritance for us,
    The excellence of Jacob whom He loves. Selah

Psalm 47:1–4

Therefore watch, and remember that for three years I did not cease to warn everyone night and day with tears.

"So now, brethren, I commend you to God and to the word of His grace, which is able to build you up and give you an inheritance among all those who are sanctified."

Acts 20:31–32

And this I say, that the law, which was four hundred and thirty years later, cannot annul the covenant that was confirmed before by God in Christ, that it should make the promise of no effect. For if the inheritance is of the law, it is no longer of promise; but God gave it to Abraham by promise.

Galatians 3:17–18

God Promises Your . . .

Hope

For You are my hope, O LORD God;
   You are my trust from my youth.
By You I have been upheld from birth;
   You are He who took me out of my mother's womb.
   My praise shall be continually of You.

Psalm 71:5–6

Thus God, determining to show more abundantly to the heirs of promise the immutability of His counsel, confirmed it by an oath, that by two immutable things, in which it is impossible for God to lie, we might have strong consolation, who have fled for refuge to lay hold of the hope set before us.

This hope we have as an anchor of the soul, both sure and steadfast, and which enters the Presence behind the veil, where the forerunner has entered for us, even Jesus, having become High Priest forever according to the order of Melchizedek.

Hebrews 6:17–20

Therefore, having been justified by faith, we have peace with God through our Lord Jesus Christ, through whom also we have access by faith into this grace in which we stand, and rejoice in hope of the glory of God.

Romans 5:1–2

I, therefore, the prisoner of the Lord, beseech you to walk worthy of the calling with which you were called, with all lowliness and gentleness, with longsuffering, bearing with one another in love, endeavoring to keep the unity of the Spirit in the bond of peace. There is one body and one Spirit, just as you were called in one hope of your calling; one Lord, one faith, one baptism; one God and Father of all, who is above all, and through all, and in you all.

Ephesians 4:1–6

But sanctify the Lord God in your hearts, and always be ready to give a defense to everyone who asks you a reason for the hope that is in you, with meekness and fear; having a good conscience, that when they defame you as evildoers, those who revile your good conduct in Christ may be ashamed. For it is better, if it is the will of God, to suffer for doing good than for doing evil.

1 Peter 3:15–17

Behold what manner of love the Father has bestowed on us, that we should be called children of God! Therefore the world does not know us, because it did not know Him. Beloved, now we are children of God; and it has not yet been revealed what we shall be, but we know that when He is revealed, we shall be like Him, for we shall see Him as He is. And everyone who has this hope in Him purifies himself, just as He is pure.

1 John 3:1–3

Blessed be the God and Father of our Lord Jesus Christ, who according to His abundant mercy has begotten us again to a living hope through the resurrection of Jesus Christ from the dead, to an inheritance incorruptible and undefiled and that does not fade away, reserved in heaven for you, who are kept by the power of God through faith for salvation ready to be revealed in the last time.

1 Peter 1:3–5

God Promises Your . . .

Praise

While I live I will praise the LORD;
  I will sing praises to my God while I have my being.
Do not put your trust in princes,
  Nor in a son of man, in whom there is no help.

Psalm 146:2–3

Let them praise the name of the LORD,
  For He commanded and they were created.
He also established them forever and ever;
  He made a decree which shall not pass away.

Psalm 148:5–6

Praise the LORD!
  Praise God in His sanctuary;
  Praise Him in His mighty firmament!
Praise Him for His mighty acts;
  Praise Him according to His excellent greatness! . . .
Let everything that has breath praise the LORD.
  Praise the LORD!

Psalm 150:1–2, 6

I will praise You, O Lᴏʀᴅ, with my whole heart;
      I will tell of all Your marvelous works.
I will be glad and rejoice in You;
      I will sing praise to Your name, O Most High.

Psalm 9:1–2

Therefore judge nothing before the time, until the Lord comes, who will both bring to light the hidden things of darkness and reveal the counsels of the hearts. Then each one's praise will come from God.

1 Corinthians 4:5

I will bless the Lᴏʀᴅ at all times;
    His praise shall continually be in my mouth.
My soul shall make its boast in the Lᴏʀᴅ;
    The humble shall hear of it and be glad.
Oh, magnify the Lᴏʀᴅ with me,
    And let us exalt His name together.

Psalm 34:1–3

The poor shall eat and be satisfied;
   Those who seek Him will praise the LORD.
   Let your heart live forever!
All the ends of the world
   Shall remember and turn to the LORD,
   And all the families of the nations
   Shall worship before You.

Psalm 22:26–27

For he is not a Jew who is one outwardly nor is circumcision that which is outward in the flesh; but he is a Jew who is one inwardly; and circumcision is that of the heart, in the Spirit, not in the letter; whose praise is not from men but from God.

Romans 2:28–29

"Praise the LORD, all your Gentiles!
Laud Him, all you peoples!"

Romans 15:11

I will sing to the LORD as long as I live;
   I will sing praise to my God while I have my being.
May my meditation be sweet to Him;
   I will be glad in the LORD.
May sinners be consumed from the earth,
   And the wicked be no more.
   Bless the LORD, O my soul!
   Praise the LORD!

Psalm 104:33–35

Encouraging Words

Encouraging words that are never spoken
   result in a life that is sometimes broken.

So make it your mission to tell someone today
   how God wants to bless them in His own special way.

Encouraging words are like flowers growing;
   when cared for and watered, you can see beauty unfolding.

—Jack Countryman

God Promises Your . . .

Joy

If you keep My commandments, you will abide in My love, just as I have kept My Father's commandments and abide in His love.

"These things I have spoken to you, that My joy may remain in you, and that your joy may be full.

John 15:10–11

Rejoice in the Lord always. Again I will say, rejoice!
Let your gentleness be known to all men. The Lord is at hand.

Philippians 4:4–5

Yet I will rejoice in the LORD,
    I will joy in the God of my salvation.
The LORD God is my strength;
    He will make my feet like deer's feet,
    And He will make me walk on my high hills.
To the Chief Musician. With my stringed instruments.

Habakkuk 3:18–19

In this you greatly rejoice, though now for a little while, if need be, you have been grieved by various trials, that the genuineness of your faith, being much more precious than gold that perishes, though it is tested by fire, may be found to praise, honor, and glory at the revelation of Jesus Christ, whom having not seen you love. Though now you do not see Him, yet believing, you rejoice with joy inexpressible and full of glory, receiving the end of your faith—the salvation of your souls.

1 Peter 1:6–9

My brethren, count it all joy when you fall into various trials, knowing that the testing of your faith produces patience.

James 1:2–3

His lord said to him, "Well done, good and faithful servant; you were faithful over a few things, I will make you ruler over many things. Enter into the joy of your lord."

Matthew 25:21

God Promises Your . . .

Servanthood

"And now, Israel, what does the Lord your God require of you, but to fear the Lord your God, to walk in all His ways and to love Him, to serve the Lord your God with all your heart and with all your soul."

Deuteronomy 10:12

And if it seems evil to you to serve the Lord, choose for yourselves this day whom you will serve, whether the gods which your fathers served that were on the other side of the River, or the gods of the Amorites, in whose land you dwell. But as for me and my house, we will serve the Lord."

So the people answered and said: "Far be it from us that we should forsake the Lord to serve other gods; for the Lord our God is He who brought us and our fathers up out of the land of Egypt, from the house of bondage, who did those great signs in our sight, and preserved us in all the way that we went and among all the people through whom we passed. And the Lord drove out from before us all the people, including the Amorites who dwelt in the land. We also will serve the Lord, for He is our God."

Joshua 24:15–18

Then Samuel said to the people, "Do not fear. You have done all this wickedness; yet do not turn aside from following the Lord, but serve the Lord with all your heart. . . . For the Lord will not forsake His people, for His great name's sake, because it has pleased the Lord to make you His people. Moreover, as for me, far be it from me that I should sin against the Lord in ceasing to pray for you; but I will teach you the good and the right way. Only fear the Lord, and serve Him in truth with all your heart; for consider what great things He has done for you."

1 Samuel 12:20, 22–24

But Jesus called them to Himself and said, "You know that the rulers of the Gentiles lord it over them, and those who are great exercise authority over them. Yet it shall not be so among you; but whoever desires to become great among you, let him be your servant. And whoever desires to be first among you, let him be your slave—just as the Son of Man did not come to be served, but to serve, and to give His life a ransom for many."

Matthew 20:25–28

And a servant of the Lord must not quarrel but be gentle to all, able to teach, patient, in humility correcting those who are in opposition, if God perhaps will grant them repentance, so that they may know the truth,

2 Timothy 2:24–25

Make a joyful shout to the LORD, all you lands!
Serve the LORD with gladness;
  Come before His presence with singing.
Know that the LORD, He is God;
  It is He who has made us, and not we ourselves;
  We are His people and the sheep of His pasture.
Enter into His gates with thanksgiving,
  And into His courts with praise.
  Be thankful to Him, and bless His name.
For the LORD is good;
  His mercy is everlasting,
  And His truth endures to all generations.

Psalm 100:1–5

But if you bite and devour one another, beware lest you be consumed by one another!

Galatians 5:15

God Promises Your . . .

Reward

If your enemy is hungry, give him bread to eat;
　　And if he is thirsty, give him water to drink;
For so you will heap coals of fire on his head,
　　And the LORD will reward you.

Proverbs 25:21–22

Behold, the LORD GOD shall come with a strong hand,
　　And His arm shall rule for Him;
　　Behold, His reward is with Him,
　　And His work before Him.
He will feed His flock like a shepherd;
　　He will gather the lambs with His arm,
　　And carry them in His bosom,
　　And gently lead those who are with young.

Isaiah 40:10–11

The fear of the LORD is clean, enduring forever;
    The judgments of the LORD are true and righteous
        altogether.
More to be desired are they than gold,
    Yea, than much fine gold;
    Sweeter also than honey and the honeycomb.
Moreover by them Your servant is warned,
    And in keeping them there is great reward.

Psalm 19:9–11

The wicked man does deceptive work,
    But he who sows righteousness will have a sure reward.
As righteousness leads to life,
    So he who pursues evil pursues it to his own death.

Proverbs 11:18–19

Now he who plants and he who waters are one, and each one will receive his own reward according to his own labor.

For we are God's fellow workers; you are God's field, you are God's building. According to the grace of God which was given to me, as a wise master builder I have laid the foundation, and another builds on it. But let each one take heed how he builds on it.

1 Corinthians 3:8–10

Look to yourselves, that we do not lose those things we worked for, but that we may receive a full reward.

Whoever transgresses and does not abide in the doctrine of Christ does not have God. He who abides in the doctrine of Christ has both the Father and the Son.

2 John 8–9

And if you do good to those who do good to you, what credit is that to you? For even sinners do the same. And if you lend to those from whom you hope to receive back, what credit is that to you? For even sinners lend to sinners to receive as much back. But love your enemies, do good, and lend, hoping for nothing in return; and your reward will be great, and you will be sons of the Most High. For He is kind to the unthankful and evil. Therefore be merciful, just as your Father also is merciful.

Luke 6:33–36

Let no one cheat you of your reward, taking delight in false humility and worship of angels, intruding into those things which he has not seen, vainly puffed up by his fleshly mind, and not holding fast to the Head, from whom all the body, nourished and knit together by joints and ligaments, grows with the increase that is from God.

Colossians 2:18–19

God Promises Your . . .

Empowerment

"Most assuredly, I say to you, he who believes in Me, the works that I do he will do also; and greater works than these he will do, because I go to My Father. And whatever you ask in My name, that I will do, that the Father may be glorified in the Son. If you ask anything in My name, I will do it."

John 14:12–14

Be anxious for nothing, but in everything by prayer and supplication, with thanksgiving, let your requests be made known to God; and the peace of God, which surpasses all understanding, will guard your hearts and minds through Christ Jesus.

Philippians 4:6–7

Is anyone among you sick? Let him call for the elders of the church, and let them pray over him, anointing him with oil in the name of the Lord. And the prayer of faith will save the sick, and the Lord will raise him up. And if he has committed sins, he will be forgiven.

James 5:14–15

"Call to Me, and I will answer you, and show you great and mighty things, which you do not know."

Jeremiah 33:3

Therefore I say to you, whatever things you ask when you pray, believe that you receive them, and you will have them.

"And whenever you stand praying, if you have anything against anyone, forgive him, that your Father in heaven may also forgive you your trespasses."

Mark 11:24–25

Above all, taking the shield of faith with which you will be able to quench all the fiery darts of the wicked one. And take the helmet of salvation, and the sword of the Spirit, which is the word of God; praying always with all prayer and supplication in the Spirit, being watchful to this end with all perseverance and supplication for all the saints.

Ephesians 6:16–18

God Promises Your . . .

Fruitfulness

"I am the true vine, and My Father is the vinedresser. Every branch in Me that does not bear fruit He takes away; and every branch that bears fruit He prunes, that it may bear more fruit."

John 15:1–2

But these are the ones sown on good ground, those who hear the word, accept it, and bear fruit: some thirtyfold, some sixty, and some a hundred.

Mark 4:20

"I am the vine, you are the branches. He who abides in Me, and I in him, bears much fruit; for without Me you can do nothing. If anyone does not abide in Me, he is cast out as a branch and is withered; and they gather them and throw them into the fire, and they are burned. If you abide in Me, and My words abide in you, you will ask what you desire, and it shall be done for you."

John 15:5–7

Even so, every good tree bears good fruit, but a bad tree bears bad fruit. A good tree cannot bear bad fruit, nor can a bad tree bear good fruit. Every tree that does not bear good fruit is cut down and thrown into the fire. Therefore by their fruits you will know them.

Matthew 7:17–20

But the fruit of the Spirit is love, joy, peace, longsuffering, kindness, goodness, faithfulness, gentleness, self-control. Against such there is no law. And those who are Christ's have crucified the flesh with its passions and desires. If we live in the Spirit, let us also walk in the Spirit. Let us not become conceited, provoking one another, envying one another.

Galatians 5:22–26

Therefore, my brethren, you also have become dead to the law through the body of Christ, that you may be married to another—to Him who was raised from the dead, that we should bear fruit to God.

Romans 7:4

You did not choose Me, but I chose you and appointed you that you should go and bear fruit, and that your fruit should remain, that whatever you ask the Father in My name He may give you.

John 15:16

God Promises Your . . .

Humility

For thus says the High and Lofty One
    Who inhabits eternity, whose name is Holy:
    "I dwell in the high and holy place,
    With him who has a contrite and humble spirit,
    To revive the spirit of the humble,
    And to revive the heart of the contrite ones."

Isaiah 57:15

But He gives more grace. Therefore He says:
    "God resists the proud,
    But gives grace to the humble."

Therefore submit to God. Resist the devil and he will flee from you. Draw near to God and He will draw near to you. Cleanse your hands, you sinners; and purify your hearts, you double-minded.

James 4:6–8

By humility and the fear of the LORD
    Are riches and honor and life.

Proverbs 22:4

Likewise you younger people, submit yourselves to your elders. Yes, all of you be submissive to one another, and be clothed with humility, for

"God resists the proud,
But gives grace to the humble."

Therefore humble yourselves under the mighty hand of God, that He may exalt you in due time, casting all your care upon Him, for He cares for you.

1 Peter 5:5–7

The LORD lifts up the humble;
He casts the wicked down to the ground.
Sing to the LORD with thanksgiving;
Sing praises on the harp to our God,
Who covers the heavens with clouds,
Who prepares rain for the earth,
Who makes grass to grow on the mountains.

Psalm 147:6–8

Therefore, as the elect of God, holy and beloved, put on tender mercies, kindness, humility, meekness, longsuffering; bearing with one another, and forgiving one another, if anyone has a complaint against another; even as Christ forgave you, so you also must do.

Colossians 3:12–13

God Promises Your . . .

Courage

Be strong and of good courage, for to this people you shall divide as an inheritance the land which I swore to their fathers to give them. Only be strong and very courageous, that you may observe to do according to all the law which Moses My servant commanded you; do not turn from it to the right hand or to the left, that you may prosper wherever you go. This Book of the Law shall not depart from your mouth, but you shall meditate in it day and night, that you may observe to do according to all that is written in it. For then you will make your way prosperous, and then you will have good success.

Joshua 1:6–8

"Be strong and courageous; do not be afraid nor dismayed before the king of Assyria, nor before all the multitude that is with him; for there are more with us than with him. With him is an arm of flesh; but with us is the Lᴏʀᴅ our God, to help us and to fight our battles." And the people were strengthened by the words of Hezekiah king of Judah.

2 Chronicles 32:7–8

Wait on the LORD;
  Be of good courage,
  And He shall strengthen your heart;
  Wait, I say, on the LORD!

Psalm 27:14

"Arise, for this matter is your responsibility. We also are with you. Be of good courage, and do it."

Then Ezra arose, and made the leaders of the priests, the Levites, and all Israel swear an oath that they would do according to this word. So they swore an oath.

Ezra 10:4–5

As the Father knows Me, even so I know the Father; and I lay down My life for the sheep. And other sheep I have which are not of this fold; them also I must bring, and they will hear My voice; and there will be one flock and one shepherd.

"Therefore My Father loves Me, because I lay down My life that I may take it again. No one takes it from Me, but I lay it down of Myself. I have power to lay it down, and I have power to take it again. This command I have received from My Father."

John 10:15–18

Then Jesus came with them to a place called Gethsemane, and said to the disciples, "Sit here while I go and pray over there." And He took with Him Peter and the two sons of Zebedee, and He began to be sorrowful and deeply distressed. Then He said to them, "My soul is exceedingly sorrowful, even to death. Stay here and watch with Me."

He went a little farther and fell on His face, and prayed, saying, "O My Father, if it is possible, let this cup pass from Me; nevertheless, not as I will, but as You will."

Matthew 26:36–39

God Promises Your . . .

Heart

Search me, O God, and know my heart;
   Try me, and know my anxieties;
And see if there is any wicked way in me,
   And lead me in the way everlasting.

Psalm 139:23–24

But the LORD said to Samuel, "Do not look at his appearance or at his physical stature, because I have refused him. For the Lord does not see as man sees; for man looks at the outward appearance, but the LORD looks at the heart."

1 Samuel 16:7

With my whole heart I have sought You;
   Oh, let me not wander from Your commandments!
Your word I have hidden in my heart,
   That I might not sin against You.
Blessed are You, O LORD!
   Teach me Your statutes.

Psalm 119:10–12

Praise the LORD!
    I will praise the LORD with my whole heart,
    In the assembly of the upright and in the congregation.
The works of the LORD are great,
    Studied by all who have pleasure in them.
His work is honorable and glorious,
    And His righteousness endures forever.
He has made His wonderful works to be remembered;
    The LORD is gracious and full of compassion.

Psalm 111:1–4

For I will set My eyes on them for good, and I will bring them back to this land; I will build them and not pull them down, and I will plant them and not pluck them up. Then I will give them a heart to know Me, that I am the LORD; and they shall be My people, and I will be their God, for they shall return to Me with their whole heart.

Jeremiah 24:6–7

Trust in the LORD with all your heart,
    And lean not on your own understanding;
In all your ways acknowledge Him,
    And He shall direct your paths.

Proverbs 3:5–6

God Promises Your . . .

Desire

Whom have I in heaven but You?
    And there is none upon earth that I desire besides You.
My flesh and my heart fail;
    But God is the strength of my heart and my portion for-
ever.

Psalm 73:25–26

You open Your hand
    And satisfy the desire of every living thing.
The LORD is righteous in all His ways,
    Gracious in all His works.
The LORD is near to all who call upon Him,
    To all who call upon Him in truth.

Psalm 145:16–18

Delight yourself also in the LORD,
    And He shall give you the desires of your heart.

Psalm 37:4

The fear of the wicked will come upon him,
   And the desire of the righteous will be granted.
When the whirlwind passes by, the wicked is no more,
   But the righteous has an everlasting foundation.

Proverbs 10:24–25

Yes, in the way of Your judgments,
   O Lord, we have waited for You;
   The desire of our soul is for Your name
   And for the remembrance of You.
With my soul I have desired You in the night,
   Yes, by my spirit within me I will seek You early;
   For when Your judgments are in the earth,
   The inhabitants of the world will learn righteousness.

Isaiah 26:8–9

Therefore, laying aside all malice, all deceit, hypocrisy, envy, and all evil speaking, as newborn babes, desire the pure milk of the word, that you may grow thereby, if indeed you have tasted that the Lord is gracious.

1 Peter 2:1–3

For this reason we also, since the day we heard it, do not cease to pray for you, and to ask that you may be filled with the knowledge of His will in all wisdom and spiritual understanding.

Colossians 1:9

To the *Teacher*

The lives you have been given
    to nurture and develop
    are fragile and tender
    and filled with great wonder.
They are just like a sponge
    soaking up knowledge and learning,
    filled with numerous questions
    which all must be answered.
Guide carefully these jewels
    you have been given.
Open their minds and let them discover
    what precious gifts they are.
God has given you the opportunity
    to change the world
    one life at a time.

—*Jack Countryman*